Follow Me Around™
Egypt

By Wiley Blevins

Content Consultant:
Noha Radwan, PhD
Associate Professor of Arabic and Comparative Literature
University of California, Davis

Library of Congress Cataloging-in-Publication Data
Names: Blevins, Wiley, author.
Title: Egypt / by Wiley Blevins.
Description: New York, NY : Children's Press, an imprint of Scholastic Inc., 2018. |
Series: Follow me around | Includes bibliographical references and index.
Identifiers: LCCN 2017058254| ISBN 9780531129203 (library binding) | ISBN 9780531138625 (pbk.)
Subjects: LCSH: Egypt—Juvenile literature. | Egypt—Description and travel—Juvenile literature.
Classification: LCC DT56.2 .B55 2018 | DDC 962—dc23
LC record available at https://lccn.loc.gov/2017058254

Design: Judith Christ & Anna Tunick Tabachnik
Text: Wiley Blevins
© 2019 Scholastic Inc.

1 2 3 4 5 6 7 8 9 10 R 28 27 26 25 24 23 22 21 20 19

Photos ©: cover background: Jon Arnold/AWL Images; cover children: PhotoAlto/Anne-Sophie Bost/Getty Images; back cover: PhotoAlto/Anne-Sophie Bost/Getty Images; 3: Izanbar/Dreamstime; 4 top left background: Thomas Wyness/Dreamstime; 4 children: PhotoAlto/Anne-Sophie Bost/Getty Images; 6 left: Sylvain Grandadam/age fotostock; 6 right: Eric TEISSEDRE/Getty Images; 7 top left: trappy76/Shutterstock; 7 bottom right: Bartosz Hadyniak/iStockphoto; 8 top left: Allstar/age fotostock; 8 top right: Curioso/Shutterstock; 8 bottom: Paul Cowan/Dreamstime; 9 top left: Alexander Mychko/Dreamstime; 9 center left bottom: AS Food studio/Shutterstock; 9 bottom left: George Nazmi Bebawi/Shutterstock; 9 center left top: nabil refaat/Shutterstock; 9 bottom right: posteriori/iStockphoto; 10: Mohamed Elraai/AP Images; 11 left: Richard Baker/In Pictures/Getty Images; 11 right: kamomeen/Shutterstock; 12 left: gmast3r/iStockphoto; 12 right: gmast3r/iStockphoto; 12 -13 background: Vadim Yerofeyev/Dreamstime; 13 left: Andy Bridge/Getty Images; 13 right: heywoody/iStockphoto; 14 top left: eFesenko/Shutterstock; 14 top right: oversnap/iStockphoto; 14 bottom: Robert Harding Productions/age fotostock; 15 left: S Tauqueur/age fotostock; 15 right: gbarm/iStockphoto; 16 top left: NaLha/iStockphoto; 16 top right: zbg2/iStockphoto; 16 bottom: The Print Collector/age fotostock; 17 right: Fine Art Images/Heritage Images/Getty Images; 17 left: Calavision/Shutterstock; 18 left: World History Archive/Alamy Images; 18 center: markgoddard/iStockphoto; 18 right: Sarin Images/The Granger Collection; 19 left: Historica Graphica Collection/Heritage Images/Getty Images; 19 center left: DEA/G. DAGLI ORTI/Getty Images; 19 center right: Paul Fearn/Alamy Images; 19 right: Tara Todras-Whitehill/AP Images; 20 top left: Denis_prof/iStockphoto; 20 top center: Matthijs Kuijpers/Dreamstime; 20 top right: Suriya KK/Shutterstock; 20 bottom left: Danilo Mongiello/Dreamstime; 20 bottom right: Tolga_TEZCAN/iStockphoto; 20 center right: Pixelrobot/Dreamstime; 21 right: Images by Itani/Alamy Images; 21 center: swisshippo/iStockphoto; 21 left: DEA/G DAGLI ORTI/age fotostock; 22: Ahmed Gomaa/Xinhua/Alamy Images; 23 top: Xinhua/Ahmed Gomaa/Getty Images; 23 center: Mohamed Abd El Ghany/Reuters; 23 bottom: Hassan Ammar/AP Images; 24: Amr Abdallah Dalsh/Reuters; 25 left: Franz-Marc Frei/Getty Images; 25 center: Fotokon/Shutterstock; 25 right: MikeDotta/Shutterstock; 26 top left: Toño Labra/age fotostock; 26 top right: DEA/S. VANNINI/De Agostini/Getty Images; 26 bottom: somedocu/Shutterstock; 27 bottom right: Paul Fleet/Shutterstock; 27 top right: Izanbar/Dreamstime; 27 bottom left: KHALED DESOUKI/AFP/Getty Images; 27 top left: Jon Arnold/AWL Images; 28 G.: Andrey Nekrasov/age fotostock; 28 A.: De Agostini/A. Dagli Orti/age fotostock; 28 B.: Ahmed Gomaa/Xinhua/Alamy Images; 28 F.: unterwegs/Shutterstock; 28 C.: Amr Nabil/AP Images; 28 E.: Edwardgerges/Dreamstime; 29: thumb/iStockphoto; 30 top right: flowgraph/iStockphoto; 30 top left: Leontura/iStockphoto; 30 bottom: PhotoAlto/Anne-Sophie Bost/Getty Images.

Maps by Jim McMahon/Mapman ®.

Table of Contents

Where in the World Is Egypt?

Ahlan wa sahlan (AH-hluhn WA SAH-hluhn) from Egypt! That's how we say "hello and welcome." We are Marwa and Hazem, your tour guides. We're sister and brother. Welcome to our fascinating and historic country. You'll see pyramids, **mummies**, and more!

Most of Egypt is in northeastern Africa. One section, the Sinai **Peninsula**, crosses into Asia. Egypt is part of a region in the world known as the Middle East. Our country is covered with deserts. So there are many hot and interesting places to visit. Let's go!

Fast Facts:

- Egypt covers 386,662 square miles (1,001,450 square kilometers).

- Egypt shares a border with Sudan to the south, Libya to the west, and Israel to the east. The Red Sea also lies to the east. The Mediterranean Sea forms Egypt's northern border.

- Egypt's famous river, the Nile, is the longest river in the world at 4,175 miles (6,719 km). It flows north and empties into the Mediterranean Sea.

- Deserts cover more than 90 percent of Egypt. The Western, or Libyan, Desert is part of the Sahara Desert. The Eastern, or Arabian, Desert lies east of the Nile River.

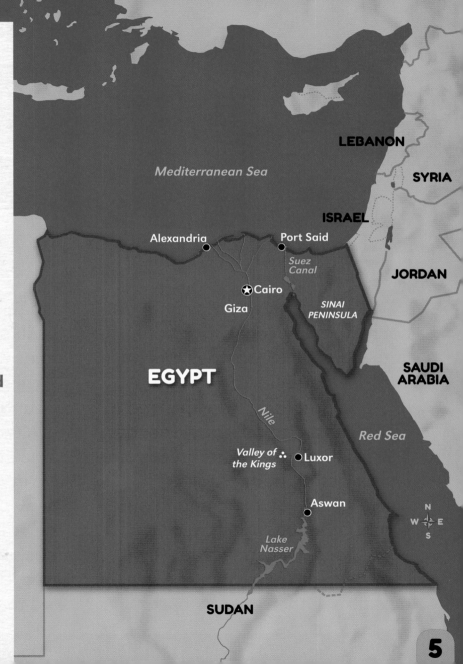

LEBANON

SYRIA

Mediterranean Sea

ISRAEL

Alexandria

Port Said

Suez Canal

JORDAN

★Cairo

Giza

SINAI PENINSULA

EGYPT

SAUDI ARABIA

Nile

Red Sea

Valley of the Kings

Luxor

Aswan

N W E S

Lake Nasser

SUDAN

5

Cairo

Home Sweet Home

We are from Cairo, Egypt. In our country, many **generations** of a family often live together. We live with our parents, older brother, and grandmother in an apartment. Egyptians are usually very friendly. Don't be surprised if we greet you with a kiss on both cheeks.

We'll take you exploring in our neighborhood. But be warned. *Beep! Beep!* Our streets are *very* crowded with cars. Many people take taxis. Others rely on buses and the Metro. The Metro is our local train system. There are also trains that run outside the city. In **rural** areas, some people get around by camel and donkey.

Although our family lives in a large city, about half of all Egyptians live in rural, or country, villages. Many of the people in this part of the country are farmers. Egypt's most important crop is cotton. It is used in making clothes, blankets, and many other products.

Nubian house

Farmers also grow oranges, rice, dates, and sugarcane. Most homes in the country are made of mud or brick. They might look simple on the outside, but they are often quite colorful inside. For example, you might see large decorative cushions. These are used for seating.

In Egypt, we work and go to school from Sunday through Thursday. Friday and Saturday are our weekend. That's because we go to the **mosque** to pray on Friday.

Ways We Dress

We dress in a very **modest** way in Egypt. We often cover our arms and legs. Men might wear a long-sleeved robe called a *jalabiyyah* (jeh-luh-BEE-yuh) or a long-sleeved shirt and long pants. Women often wear a robe called an *abaya* (uh-BAY-yah), with a scarf, or *hijab* (hih-JAHB), over their hair. Some people wear Western-style clothes such as jeans and long-sleeved shirts.

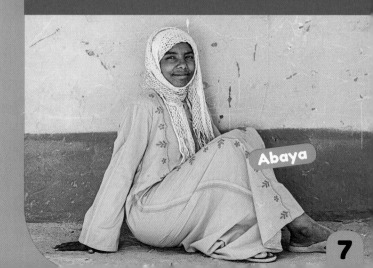

Abaya

7

Street stall

Dates

Let's Eat!

When it comes to food, we like to share and eat together! Breakfast is often *fuul* (FOOL). That's stewed fava beans. Lunch is our main meal. We eat at about 2 o'clock. The two of us really like *koshari* (KUSH-ar-ee). It has pasta, rice, lentils, chickpeas, and onions. All of this is topped with spicy tomato sauce. It's so good! For dinner, we usually eat leftovers from lunch. Sometimes, we have *molokhia* (mul-oo-KHEE-yuh), a spicy vegetable soup. We often dip pita or other bread into soups and stews. It's the best way to eat! Other salty foods include *shawarma* (shuh-WAHR-muh), which is shaved meat and vegetables. *Falafel* (feh-LAH-ful) is fried chickpea patties. We don't eat much meat in Egypt, though. And, because our family is Muslim, we do not eat pork.

Fuul

For dessert, you should try *um ali* (OOM ah-LEE). This sweet treat is made from pastry, cream, coconut, raisins, and nuts. We also eat a lot of dates in our country. Egypt is the largest producer in the world of this tasty fruit.

For a drink, we love to have a special tea called *shai* (SHY). It is made with mint leaves. There is also a drink made from hibiscus flowers called *karkade* (kar-kah-DAY). We drink a lot of milk, too. It might come from goats, sheep, or even buffaloes. Our parents drink *ahwa* (AH-hwah), or coffee, and coffee shops are quite popular here. You'll also see men smoking a special water pipe called a *shisha* (SHEE-shuh) while there.

Koshari

Molokhia

Falafel

Um ali

A Full Plate

We want our guests to enjoy their meals. A good host will keep your plate at least half full at all times. But don't feel like you have to keep eating! We're just worried you are still hungry. Always say *"teslam iidak"* (te-SLAHM ih-DAHK) to your host. That means "Bless your hands" and is a nice compliment.

Shawarma

9

Off to School

In Egypt, we go to school from ages 6 to 14. The first thing you'll notice about our classroom is how crowded it is. But even though there are a lot of kids in our class, we get to sit next to our best *asdiqa'* (uhs-dee-KAH-ih), or friends. After elementary school, about half of all students go on to high school. From there, about 20 percent go to college. We both hope to go to Cairo or Alexandria University. Egypt is also home to the world's oldest university, Al-Azhar. It was started in 970 CE!

We study subjects such as math, history, and religion in school. Egypt's most common religion is Islam.

One of the main things we learn in school is how to read and write Arabic, Egypt's official language. We also learn some English and French, which a lot of people speak here.

أصدقاء
(asdiqa')
friends

Some kids study the Quran, Islam's holy book, at a religious school.

Our alphabet, the Arabic alphabet, has 28 letters. It is the second most used alphabet in the world. The first is the Latin alphabet, which is what you use in English. Arabic is written from right to left. That is the opposite of how English is written!

More than one-fourth of all Egyptians cannot read and write. But we are working hard to improve our schools. We'd both like to be teachers when we grow up.

Knowing how to count to 10 is important if you visit Egypt.

Also, pay attention to how the numbers are written.

 1   **wahed** (WEH-hed)

 2   **ethnein** (ith-NAYN)

 3   **thalaatha** (theh-LEH-thah)

 4   **arba'a** (ahr-BA-ah)

 5   **khamsa** (KHUM-suh)

 6   **sitta** (SIT-uh)

 7   **sab'aa** (SUB-ah)

 8   **thamaniya** (them-EHN-ee-yuh)

 9   **tis'aa** (TIZ-ah)

 10   **ashara** (AH-shuh-ruh)

11

Clever Hasan and the Ogre

In school and at home, we often hear tales of Clever Hasan. This is one of our favorite adventures of his!

There were once 10 brothers. The most handsome and clever of them was Hasan, the youngest.

One day, the nine older brothers went hunting. Hasan stayed home with their father. The brothers did not return for many weeks. Worried, Hasan went to find them. Before long, he came to an old man. "Peace to you, sir," said Hasan. "I'm looking for my brothers." "An ogre turned them to stone," said the man. "The creature lives in the palace over there. He holds a girl captive inside and keeps her hanging by her feet. She can tell you how to beat the ogre."

Hasan thanked the man and walked to the palace. When he found the captive girl, he helped her down. Grateful, she offered to help save his brothers. "The ogre's soul is in a crocodile in So-and-So's kingdom," she said. "Strike the crocodile only once to kill it. Then take the ogre's soul from the animal's belly."

Hasan went to the kingdom as the girl said. The people living there told Hasan that their princess was to be sacrificed to the crocodile.

Hasan went to the river where the princess waited for the crocodile. When the crocodile came, Hasan struck it with a sword. "Would you strike me again?" asked the crocodile. Hasan refused, and the crocodile died. Had Hasan struck again, the crocodile would have lived!

Inside the crocodile's belly were three eggs. Each was part of the ogre's soul. Hasan took them back to the ogre's palace. There, he broke one egg. The ogre appeared. Part of his body was very broken. "What have you done?" yelled the ogre.

"Your soul is in my hands," Hasan said. "Free my brothers."

"Take the sand beneath you and scatter it."

Hasan did so. Many people appeared, but not his brothers. "Scatter more sand!" the ogre pleaded. Hasan did. More people appeared, but not his brothers. Hasan scattered another handful. Finally! His brothers appeared.

"Are there more people in this sand?" Hasan asked. The ogre nodded. Angry, Hasan broke the final two eggs. The ogre died. Then Hasan scattered the rest of the sand, freeing everyone. Everyone went home happy, including Clever Hasan and his brothers.

Khân al-Khalîlî

Most people in Egypt live near the Nile River.

Touring Egypt

Cairo: Capital City

Welcome to our city, Cairo. It's the capital of Egypt. Like many of our country's cities, it's located along the Nile River. A great place to visit is the Museum of Egyptian **Antiquities**. It has mummies, King Tut's gold mask, and more than 100,000 other ancient objects. You can spend all day there! We go a couple of times a year.

Another must-stop is the maze-like Khân al-Khalîlî, an outdoor bazaar. A bazaar is a market. You can grab a quick snack or buy souvenirs. Be ready to **haggle** for the best price! Nearby is Fishawi's Café, run by the same family for almost 250 years! It's a perfect spot to sip some mint tea. Then head to Al-Azhar Park. It's one of the most beautiful parts of Cairo.

King Tut's mask

The pyramids at Giza are surrounded by desert.

The Great Sphinx

Giza

Egypt is most famous for one thing—pyramids! Egyptians started building them about 4,500 years ago. The largest pyramid is about 450 feet (137 meters) tall. It is called the Great Pyramid and is located in Giza, just outside of Cairo. The Great Pyramid was built as a tomb, or burial place, for Khufu, a pharaoh. Pharaoh is what ancient Egyptian rulers were called. Two other large pyramids stand nearby. These were tombs for other pharaohs. People also built monuments to honor pharaohs. One of our favorite monuments in Giza is the Great Sphinx. It has the head of a pharaoh and the body of a lion. It is so big that its eyes are 6 feet (2 m) tall. That's way taller than either of us! The best way to reach the Sphinx is by camel. Hop on and enjoy the bumpy ride.

Suez Canal

Karnak Temple

Alexandria

Head north to Alexandria. We call this city the Pearl of the Mediterranean. Greek leader Alexander the Great built it thousands of years ago. He named it after himself. Today, Alexandria is our most important **port** city. The famous Lighthouse of Alexandria once stood here. Ancient writers called it one of the Seven Wonders of the World.

Lighthouse of Alexandria

Unfortunately, an earthquake destroyed it in 1323.

Port Said is a city that sits at the northern end of the Suez Canal. Here, you can see big boats coming in. The canal, which first opened in 1869, connects the Mediterranean Sea with the Red Sea. It is an incredibly important waterway because it creates a shortcut for ships traveling between Asia and Europe. This makes travel between these places much faster!

Valley of the Kings

Other Ancient Places

Luxor in southern Egypt is home to the Karnak Temple Complex. This is the world's largest group of religious buildings. Ride a horse-drawn cart along the Corniche. That's the main street along the Nile River in Luxor.

Nearby is the Valley of the Kings. So far, more than 60 royal tombs have been found buried in the hills there. The tomb walls are covered in amazing art. **Hieroglyphics** tell stories about the person's life. There are also prayers and messages.

Ancient Library

In ancient times, Alexandria was an important center of learning. In fact, it was home to the largest library in the world. But the library burned to the ground more than 2,000 years ago. Its destuction occurred when Roman general Julius Caesar attacked Egypt. Many one-of-a-kind books that had been inside the library were lost forever.

Our Country's History

Our country has a long and interesting history. Tourists come from all over the world to learn about our past. Pharaohs ruled Egypt for thousands of years. In all, we had 31 **<u>dynasties</u>**. Each dynasty was a series of pharaohs from the same family. The pharaohs' rule ended when the Greeks conquered our land. One of the first Greek rulers was Ptolemy. His family ruled Egypt for almost 300 years. It ended

Timeline: Key Moments in Egyptian History

Farming

Hieroglyphics

Alexander the Great

About 5000 BCE	3100 BCE	332 BCE	642 CE
Early Farmers People develop systems to bring water from sources such as the Nile River into fields for farming.	**Pharaohs** Two countries, Upper Egypt and Lower Egypt, unite into one Egypt. Pharaohs begin ruling. Hieroglyphics are invented.	**Greek Invasion** Greeks take control of Egypt under Alexander the Great. After Alexander's death in 323 BCE, Ptolemy rules.	**Arab Invasion** Arab Muslims from what is now Saudi Arabia take over. They bring Islam with them.

with the death of the famous queen Cleopatra. It is believed she killed herself with the bite of an asp, a poisonous snake. After her death, Egypt was ruled by various rulers, including Arabs, Ottomans from what is now Turkey, the French, and the British. It wasn't until the 20th century that Egypt gained its independence. We are still struggling to find which type of government and rule is best for our country.

Ottoman emperor Bayezid II

French emperor Napoleon in Giza

President Naguib

Protest in Cairo

1517

1798–1922

1922

1952

2010–Today

Ottoman Rule
The Ottoman Empire, centered in present-day Turkey, takes control of the Egyptian government.

European Invasions
Ottoman, French, and British forces fight for power in Egypt. Great Britain takes full control in 1882.

The Kingdom of Egypt
Great Britain grants Egypt independence but remains involved in its rule. A king becomes head of the country.

Egyptian Revolution
Gamal Abdel Nasser leads a revolution. Muhammad Naguib becomes Egypt's president.

Changes in Government
Egyptians protest for change and more say in their government.

It Came From Egypt

Cobra

Jerboa

Egypt's wild animals include deadly cobras, stinging scorpions, laughing hyenas, beautiful lynxes, friendly hoopoes, and elegant gazelles. We really like the jerboa. This mouse-like animal has long back legs. It uses these legs to jump around the desert. A very rare animal is the hyrax. It lives in the Sinai Peninsula. Because visitors long ago didn't know what it was, they often called it a rabbit or hare. It's not.

Papyrus plant

Ancient Egyptians didn't have paper. They used papyrus. It's a plant that grows along the Nile River. Parts of the plant are pounded into thin sheets and dried. People long ago wrote and drew on these sheets. We still make papyrus today.

Papyrus

Obelisk

Egyptians have created many inventions. These include toothbrushes, toothpaste, locks, eye makeup, irrigation, plows, obelisks (sun clocks), stitches, wigs, breath mints, bowling, and more. You can thank us later!

Hyrax

Rosetta Stone

Zoom!

Ancient Egyptians wrote using picture-symbols called hieroglyphics. Over the centuries, Egyptians started using other forms of writing. People could no longer read hieroglyphics. Then soldiers accidentally discovered a big stone tablet called the Rosetta Stone in 1799. It had a message on it in three languages. One was hieroglyphics. Researchers used the other two known languages to translate the hieroglyphics. This unlocked the code!

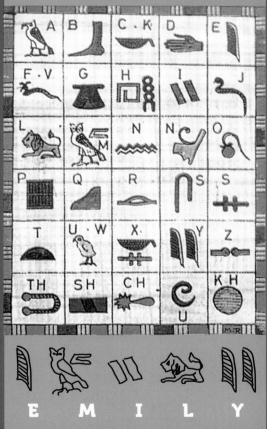

Use these hieroglyphics to write your name!

E M I L Y

Eid al-Fitr celebrations at the end of Ramadan can be a lot of fun!

Celebrate!

Everyone loves a holiday, and we have some big ones in Egypt. Most Egyptians, including our family, are Muslim. We follow Islam. Ramadan is our most important religious holiday. It lasts one month. During this time, we fast, or don't eat, from sunrise to sunset. The holiday ends with Eid al-Fitr. It's a three-day celebration. We eat a lot during these days, as well as pray and give one another gifts.

Other Celebrations

March, April

Sham-el-Nessim
This holiday's name means "smelling of the breeze." It marks the beginning of spring and dates back to the time of the pharaohs. People celebrate by going to parks, decorating eggs, and having fun.

July 23

Revolution Day
We celebrate a day in 1952 when we stood up to an unfair government. The Republic of Egypt was formed as a result of that day.

Eid al-Adha (Feast of the Sacrifice)
Many families sacrifice a sheep or goat for this special four-day holiday. Some of the meat is donated to the poor. This holiday happens at different times each year.

Five Pillars of Islam

As Egypt's most common religion, Islam plays a major part in many people's lives. The religion includes five principles, called pillars, that Muslims follow to show commitment to God. Here is a little bit about each one.

1st Pillar **Faith**
Believe in God and the Prophet Muhammed.

2nd Pillar **Prayer**
Pray each day facing the holy city of Mecca.

3rd Pillar **Charity**
Give to and help those in need.

4th Pillar **Fasting**
Don't eat or drink during the day in the holy month of Ramadan.

5th Pillar **Pilgrimage**
Visit the holy city of Mecca at least once, if you can.

23

Camel racing

Time to Play

We kids in Egypt love our sports, and soccer is our favorite. GOAL! Our family and friends gather around the TV whenever one of our best national teams plays. Everyone we know roots for either Cairo's Al-Ahly or Giza's El Zamalek. People in Egypt also love weight lifting, boxing, wrestling, basketball, handball, squash, swimming, and tennis.

Camel racing keeps growing in popularity. Each May, Egypt hosts the South Sinai Camel Festival. It features a long and bumpy camel race. Our family tries to go every year. It's our dad's favorite race.

People here also often go to outdoor markets, buy food and clothes, and just hang out with our friends. Much like you.

Oud

Rababa

When Dervishes dance as part of their worship, they wear white. When performing, however, they might wear bright colors.

Music is a big part of what we do for fun, too. The *oud* (OOD) is a stringed instrument that musicians strum and pluck. Musicians play the *rababa* (rah-BAH-bah), with a bow, like a violin. When audiences enjoy live music at restaurants, theaters, clubs, and other spots, they hum, clap, cheer, cry, or sing along. So join in!

With music, comes dancing! An old dance form called *raqs sharqi* (RAHKS SHAR-kee) is said to have started in Egypt. It is better known as belly dancing. Our favorite dancers, however, are the whirling dervishes. These spinning dancers are a sight to see! The dance started as a way to worship God. Today, it's often done as a performance.

25

You Won't Believe This!

Queen Cleopatra

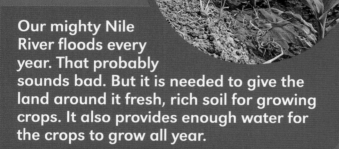

Our mighty Nile River floods every year. That probably sounds bad. But it is needed to give the land around it fresh, rich soil for growing crops. It also provides enough water for the crops to grow all year.

The palace of the famous Queen Cleopatra is now under the sea near Alexandria. Don't worry! People are working to make it into an underwater museum. Cool or scary?

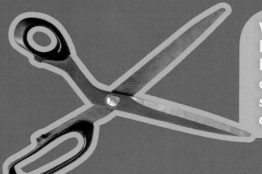

What do you think is bad luck? Some Egyptians believe owls, black cats, open scissors, and leaving shoes upside down are signs of bad luck or bad news.

Pyramids

Scientists are using NASA satellite images to find more ancient pyramids. These special scans are able to find pyramids buried long ago under dirt and sand. It seems like every year, we are discovering more about our country's past.

Mummified cat

Ancient Egyptians made lots of mummies. But not just of dead pharaohs and other royals. They also mummified cats, ibises (birds), lions, snakes, crocodiles, and other animals. In the Crocodile Museum in Kom Ombo, you can see 40 crocodile mummies. Snap!

We have a special dish made of cured fish called *fesikh* (FIH-sikh). But be careful! If it's made the right way, it's tasty. If not, it can be poisonous. Uh-oh!

Scarabs, a type of beetle, have been shown in Egyptian art for thousands of years. This bug takes dung (poo) and rolls it into balls. The ancient Egyptians thought it was like the sun god rolling the sun across the sky each day. So this beetle was sacred. Other insects were also considered special. Ancient soldiers were sometimes given flies made of gold for their bravery in battle.

Guessing Game!

Here are some other great sites around Egypt. If you visit, try to see them all!

This temple honors one of our few female pharaohs.

G

B Go to this desert oasis to visit Egypt's only waterfalls.

If you're brave, travel down into these stone rooms called catacombs. They were carved to house dead bodies.

A

F

This is one of the largest human-made lakes in the world.

Travel back 3,000 years in time at this village, which was built to re-create life in ancient Egypt.

C

D

This Red Sea fort, made of brick and stone, is rich in history.

E

Opened in 1971, this dam controls the mighty Nile River.

28

How to Prepare for Your Visit

You might have the chance to see Egypt in person someday. Here are some tips that could help you prepare for a trip.

1 Our money is called the Egyptian pound. You'll find pictures of Egyptian monuments and scenes from ancient Egyptian life on it. You'll need pounds to buy fun souvenirs.

2 It's best to not drink the local tap water. Instead, buy bottled water, even for brushing your teeth. And remember, ice cubes are made of water!

3 We have many religious sites in Egypt. Remember to take off your shoes before entering. In mosques, women must cover their head, arms, and legs. No shorts, tank tops, or leggings either. If you're not sure about the rules, please ask before you enter.

4 Visitors should sail the Nile. We recommend hopping on a *dahabiya* (dah-hah-BEE-yuh), a boat with beautiful white sails. Be sure to take pictures of the *feluccas* (feh-LOO-kuhs). These small wooden boats have traveled the Nile for centuries.

5 Egypt has two seasons. Winter is cool and usually in the 50s and 60s Fahrenheit (between 10 and 21 degrees Celsius). Summers are hot. Temperatures regularly go above 100°F (38°C). But no matter the time of year, it is dry, dry, dry!

6 Around April, we are hit with a hot, dusty wind called a *khamsin* (KHAM-seen). It creates massive dust storms. This is not the best time to visit us.

The United States Compared to Egypt

	United States of America (USA)	Arab Republic of Egypt
Official Name	United States of America (USA)	Arab Republic of Egypt
Official Language	No official language, though English is most commonly used	Arabic
Population	325 million	More than 97 million
Common Words	yes, no, please, thank you	na'am (NAH-uhm), laa (LAH), min fadlak (MIN FAHZ-lehk), shukran (SHU-krahn)
Flag		
Money	Dollar	Egyptian pound
Location	North America	Northeastern Africa; the Sinai Peninsula is in Asia
Highest Point	Denali (Mount McKinley)	Mount Catherine
Lowest Point	Death Valley	Qattara Depression
National Anthem	"The Star-Spangled Banner"	"Bilady, Laki Hubbi Wa Fu'adi"

So now you know some important and fascinating things about our country, Egypt. We hope to see you someday touring one of our ancient sites, sailing on the Nile, or enjoying a tasty traditional meal. Until then...*ma'a salama* (MAH-uh sah-LAH-mah). Good-bye.

Glossary

antiquities
(an-TIH-kwuh-teez)
objects such as coins, statues, and buildings from ancient times

dynasties
(DYE-nuh-steez)
series of rulers belonging to the same family

generations
(jen-uh-RAY-shuhnz)
groups of all the people born around the same time

haggle
(HAG-uhl)
to argue with someone, usually to agree on the price of something

hieroglyphics
(hire-uh-GLIF-iks)
a system of writing used by ancient Egyptians

modest
(MAH-dist)
not large, showy, or expensive

mosque
(MAHSK)
a building where Muslims worship

mummies
(MUH-meez)
dead bodies that have been preserved with special chemicals and wrapped in cloth

peninsula
(puh-NIN-suh-luh)
a piece of land that sticks out from a larger landmass and is almost completely surrounded by water

port
(PORT)
a town or city with a harbor where ships can dock and load or unload cargo

rural
(ROOR-uhl)
of or having to do with the countryside, country life, or farming

31

Index

Facts for Now

Visit this Scholastic website for more information on Egypt and to download the Teaching Guide for this series:

www.factsfornow.scholastic.com   Enter the keyword **Egypt**

About the Author

Wiley Blevins lives and works in New York City. His greatest love is traveling, and he has been all over the  world, including the Middle East. He has also written the Ick and Crud series and the Scary Tales Retold series.